GREAT RIVERS

The AMAZON

Michael Pollard

BENCHMARK BOOKS

MARSHALL CAVENDISH
NEW YORK

Benchmark Books
Marshall Cavendish Corporation
99 White Plains Road
Tarrytown, New York 10591

American edition © Marshall Cavendish Corporation 1998

First published in 1997 by Evans Brothers Limited
© Evans Brothers Limited 1997

Library of Congress Cataloging-in-Publication Data
Pollard, Michael, date.
    The Amazon / Michael Pollard.
        p.   cm. — (Great rivers)
    Includes bibliographical references and index.
    Summary: Describes the effects of the world's second
longest river on the history, food, economy,
transportation, plants, wildlife, and people of the region
through which it flows.
    ISBN 0-7614-0501-1 (lib. bdg.)
    1. Amazon River—Juvenile literature. [1. Amazon
River.] I. Title. II. Series: Pollard, Michael, date. Great
rivers.
F2546.P77 1998
981'.1—DC21   97-16546
                                          CIP
                                          AC

Printed in Hong Kong

ACKNOWLEDGEMENTS

For permission to reproduce copyright material, the author
and publishers gratefully acknowledge the following:

Cover (main image) Tony Morrison/South American
Pictures (bottom left) Lupe Cunha Photos (right) Kevin
Schafer/Still Pictures
Title page Andre Bartschi/Still Pictures **page 8** (top)
Martin Wendler/Still Pictures (bottom) Tony Morrison/
South American Pictures **page 9** NASA/Science Photo
Library **page 10** (top) Tom van Sant/Geosphere Project,
Santa Monica/Science Photo Library (bottom) Marion
Morrison/ South American Pictures **page 11** Johnathan
Smith/Sylvia Cordaiy Photo Library **page 12** Mary Evans
Picture Library **page 13** (top) Edward Parker/Still Pictures
(bottom) Peter Dixon/South American Pictures **page 14**
Mary Evans Picture Library **page 15** Mark Edwards/Still
Pictures **page 16** South American Pictures **page 17** Andre
Bartschi/Planet Earth Pictures **page 18** (top right)
Johnathan Smith/Sylvia Cordaiy Photo Library (middle)
Earth Satellite Corporation/Science Photo Library **page 19**
Tony Morrison/South American Pictures **page 20** Kevin
Schafer/Still Pictures **page 21** (top) Trip/W Jacobs (bottom)
Mark Edwards/ Still Pictures **page 22** Earth Satellite
Corporation/Science Photo Library **page 23** (top) Tony
Morrison/South American Pictures (bottom) Kevin
Schafer/Still Pictures **page 24** Tony Morrison/South
American Pictures **page 25** (top) K. Gillham/Robert
Harding Picture Library (bottom) Tony Morrison/South
American Pictures **page 26** (top left) Robert Harding
Picture Library (bottom right) Tony Morrison/South
American Pictures **page 27** (top) Edward Parker (bottom
right) Tony Morrison/South American Pictures **page 28**
(top) Mark Edwards/Still Pictures (bottom) Edward Parker
page 29 (right) Lupe Cunha Photos (bottom left) Andre
Bartschi/Still Pictures **page 30** Mark Edwards/Still Pictures
page 31 (top) Mark Edwards/Still Pictures (bottom) Mark
Edwards/Still Pictures **page 32** Robin Hanbury-
Tenison/Robert Harding Picture Library **page 33** Tony
Morrison/South American Pictures **page 34** Index
Editora/South American Pictures **page 35** Mark
Edwards/Still Pictures **page 36** Michael Doolittle/Still
Pictures **page 37** (top) Chris Caldicott/Still Pictures
(bottom) Mark Edwards/Still Pictures **page 38** Andre
Bartschi/Still Pictures **page 39** (top) Y. J. Rey-Millet/Still
Pictures (bottom) Andre Bartschi/Still Pictures **page 40**
(top) Mark Edwards/Still Pictures (bottom) Julio
Etchart/Reportage/Still Pictures **page 41** Mark
Edwards/Still Pictures **page 42** Mark Edwards/Still Pictures
page 43 (left and right) Mark Edwards/Still Pictures

CONTENTS

THE MIGHTY AMAZON

THE AMAZON FLOWS EASTWARDS FROM THE ANDES MOUNTAINS ON THE WESTERN SIDE OF SOUTH AMERICA ALL THE WAY ACROSS TO THE ATLANTIC OCEAN — A DISTANCE OF 3902 MILES (6280 KILOMETERS).

◀ *The Amazon near Iquitos in Peru at the start of the rainy season. In November rain falling on the Andes Mountains causes the Amazon to swell and the floodwater continues to rise until June.*

▲ *In flood, the Amazon widens to cover its banks and the islands in the middle of the river. The sediment left by the floods enriches the soil.*

IT IS THE WORLD's second longest river. Only the Nile, in Africa, is longer. But if you measure a river by the volume of water that flows along it, the Amazon is the world leader. About 20 per cent of all the water that the world's rivers pour into the oceans comes from the Amazon. It collects water from about 40 per cent of South America's land area along over 1000 tributaries, 17 of which are over 994 miles (1600 kilometers) long. From Iquitos in Peru all the way across Brazil to the Atlantic, the Amazon is between 3.7 and 6 miles (six and ten kilometers) wide. It is even wider when it is flooded.

TROPICAL RAINFOREST

The Amazon is never more than 280 miles (450 kilometers) from the Equator. For most of its course it flows through tropical rainforest – the dense jungle that is the habitat of countless species of plant and animal life. Previously unknown species are constantly being identified.

Amazonia covers an area larger than the whole of western Europe and includes parts of Ecuador, Peru, Colombia, Venezuela and Brazil.

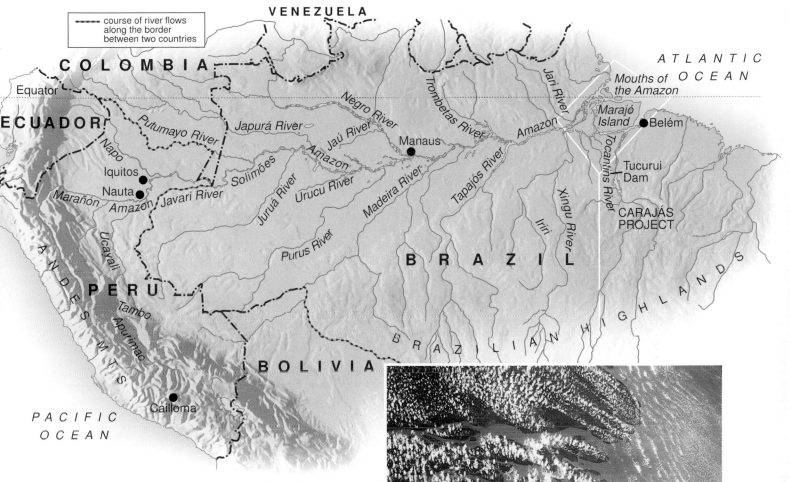

course of river flows
along the border
between two countries

VENEZUELA

COLOMBIA

ATLANTIC
OCEAN

Equator

Mouths of
the Amazon

ECUADOR

Napo

Putumayo River

Japurá River

Negro River

Jaú River

Trombetas River

Jari River

Amazon

Marajó
Island

Belém

Iquitos

Amazon

Manaus

Tocantins River

Nauta

Solimões

Javari River

Juruá River

Urucu River

Madeira River

Tapajós River

Tucurui
Dam

Marañón

Amazon

Purus River

Xingu River

CARAJÁS
PROJECT

Ucayali

Iriri

BRAZIL

PERU

Tambo

Apurímac

ANDES MTS

BOLIVIA

BRAZILIAN HIGHLANDS

Cailloma

PACIFIC
OCEAN

Yet it is one of the most sparsely populated areas of the world. Only about sixteen million people live there, which is about the same number as the population of the Netherlands. Most of them live in small, scattered settlements beside the rivers. Beyond the river banks the rainforest is so thick and difficult to travel through that many areas have never been explored or mapped.

PEOPLE OF THE AMAZON

The first people to live along the Amazon were South American Indians who arrived from the north about 10,000 years ago. They lived undisturbed until about 500 years ago when Portuguese and Spanish explorers arrived. Brazil, through which most of the Amazon flows, was then part of the Portuguese empire. It became an independent nation in 1822. Most of Brazil's development was along the coast and in the southeast of the country.

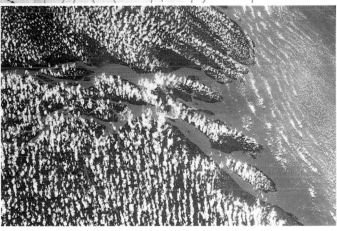

▲ The mouths of the Amazon, photographed from the US Space Shuttle Atlantis. On the right is the Atlantic Ocean, colored far out to sea by sediment from the river. Marajó Island covers most of the bottom half of the picture.

THE AMAZON

Length: 3902 mi (6280 km)
Source: Cailloma, Peru
Mouth: northeastern Brazil

It was not until the 1950s that the Brazilian government began to take an interest in the Amazon and its resources. This interest turned into a threat to the people of the forest and to its wildlife, arousing worldwide concern that one of the last great wildernesses on Earth was being destroyed.

THE MAKING OF THE AMAZON

THE MOVEMENTS IN THE EARTH'S CRUST, OR OUTER LAYER, WHICH LED TO THE MAKING OF THE AMAZON, BEGAN ABOUT 135 MILLION YEARS AGO.

IF YOU LOOK AT a map of the world, you can see how the east coast of South America and the west coast of Africa fit together like pieces of a jigsaw. Until 135 million years ago, both continents formed part of a single land that geologists call "Gondwana." Then the land began to split in two to form two continents, which we know today as South America and Africa. As the Earth's crust cooled, it split into pieces, which are called crustal plates. The South American plate, joined by a narrow neck of land to North America, moved westwards, creating the southern Atlantic Ocean to the east.

THE ANDES MOUNTAINS

About 65 million years ago, the South American plate collided with the Nazca plate, which lay beneath the Pacific Ocean. The collision caused a force that squeezed up masses of rock in great folds along the western

▶ Over 19,684 feet (6000 meters) up in the Bolivian Andes. Meltwater from the ice and snow flows into a stream. On the lower slopes of the mountains many streams like this will merge to form the Amazon.

10

◀ *This satellite photograph of South America shows how the Amazonian rainforest, colored green, stretches across the top half of the continent. The sand-colored area is desert and grassland.*

MAIN TRIBUTARIES OF THE AMAZON

Marañón, 994 mi (1600 km) joins Amazon at Nauta
Xingu, 1230 mi (1979 km) joins Amazon at Pôrto de Mos
Tapajós, 1249 mi (2010 km) joins Amazon at Santarém
Madeira, 2014 mi (3241 km) joins Amazon at Itacoatiara
Purus, 1995 mi (3211 km) joins Amazon near Anori
Tocantins, 1677 mi (2699 km) flows into Amazon delta
Juruá, 900 mi (1448 km) joins Amazon near Fonte Boa
Javari, 600 mi (966 km) joins Amazon near Leticia
Napo, 696 mi (1120 km) joins Amazon at Francisco de Orellana
Trombetas, 470 mi (756 km) joins Amazon at Óbidos
Negro, 1491 (2400 km) joins Amazon near Manaus
Japurá, 1500 mi (2414 km) joins Amazon at Foz do Copcá
Putumayo, 994 mi (1600 km) joins Amazon near Santo Antônio do Içá

edge of South America. These fold mountains became known as the Andes. Fossils of marine creatures have been found high in the Andes, which proves that they are made of rock material that was once under the sea.

THE AMAZON BASIN

When the South American and Nazca plates collided, they made shock waves like waves on the sea. The peaks of the waves formed the Andes. The dips between the waves became the deep troughs of the Pacific Ocean to the west and a depression, or hollowed-out bowl, to the east. This depression became the Amazon basin. It filled with rainwater from the mountains until it overflowed into the Atlantic. When most of the water had overflowed, the Amazon and its tributaries were left flowing across the basin.

▶ *The Amazon and its tributaries have carved out deep gorges as they flow through the mountains of Peru. Banks of sediment like the one at the bottom right make good farming land.*

THE MOUTHS OF THE AMAZON

The huge volume of water flowing down the Amazon and its tributaries carries millions of tons of sediment that is made up of fragments of rock from the mountains. As the river approaches the sea, the current slows down and the sediment is left on the river banks and the river bed. Over thousands of years, this has created a large area of muddy land at the mouth of the Amazon. The river divides and flows down a number of channels between small islands. These islands constantly change shape as the water builds up the sediment and then, in the rainy season, washes it away again. There are two main channels to the ocean and between them is the island of Marajó, which is about the same size as Denmark.

The journey of the Amazon's water does not end there. The current is still strong enough to push the river's water out into the Atlantic. It was the sight of this muddy water, 186 miles (300 kilometers) out to sea, that first led Spanish explorers to the Amazon 500 years ago.

11

THE FIRST AMAZONIANS

THE FIRST PEOPLE TO LIVE IN
SOUTH AMERICA ARRIVED
BETWEEN 15 AND 20 THOUSAND
YEARS AGO. THEY WERE THE
DESCENDANTS OF TRAVELERS
FROM ASIA WHO HAD CROSSED
THE BERING STRAIT INTO
NORTH AMERICA.

THESE TRAVELERS, or nomads, lived by hunting and gathering wild plants for food, such as wild grapes and nuts, and by keeping herds of animals. They had no settled homes. The search for food for themselves and their herds led them steadily southwards over many thousands of years. Some settled in North America. Others moved on to Mexico and the narrow neck of land that joins the two American continents and they founded communities there. Other groups went further – into South America.

SETTLING DOWN

By about 10,000 years ago people had arrived in the Amazon basin and some began to exchange their nomadic lifestyle for a more settled way of life. Some people experimented with growing instead of gathering their food. By about 1500 BC they were cultivating corn and manioc – a root vegetable that can be crushed and ground into flour. Small farming and fishing communities developed along the rivers, each developing its own customs and way of life. If the different communities needed to communicate with each other, they used the rivers for transport. Slowly,

▲ *The Amazon rainforest is the main habitat of the boa constrictor, which suffocates its prey by squeezing it. The nineteenth-century artist who drew this picture of the capture of a boa constrictor exaggerated its length, which is 9.8 feet (three meters) at most.*

neighboring communities made links through marriage or by uniting against an enemy from outside and so tribes, or "nations," were formed. They were united by their community, their culture and language. The crops they planted, the plant and animal life of the forest and the fish in the rivers provided all their food.

POISON ARROWS

Other groups preferred to live as hunter-gatherers deep in the forest. The Yanomami Indians, for example, were hunters who used bows and arrows. The arrowheads were made of sharpened monkey bones and were tipped with curare, which is a poison made from the sap of plants. By AD 1500 there are thought to have been between six and nine million

▲ *Fishing provides many villagers of the rainforest with a living. This fisherman is skinning a piraracu fish, which will feed many families for days.*

Amazonian Indians living in Amazonia. It is estimated that up to one million Amazonian Indians live in isolated communities in Amazonia today.

To the west, in the mountains of present-day Peru, the Incas founded a civilization with well-built cities linked by good roads. By AD 1500 the Incas had conquered much of the Pacific coast of South America. But they did not try to invade the Amazon basin, probably because the Andes were a difficult barrier to cross. So the people of the Amazon and its tributaries were left in peace until, one day in 1499 or 1500, a strange ship was sighted off the coast near the mouth of the Amazon.

▼ *An Asurini Indian settlement near Breves on Marajó Island. The house is built on a raft so that it will rise when the floods come. Each year, floodwater will leave a layer of sediment on the cultivated land, enriching it for the next crop.*

THE MARAJÓ ISLAND CIVILIZATION

Little is known about the early history of the Amazonian Indians, with one exception. The Indians who lived on the island of Marajó, between the two main mouths of the Amazon, learned how to make clay pottery, and examples of this have been found. The pottery has been dated to about 1500 BC. This pottery would have been made without a wheel, because the wheel was unknown in South America until it was introduced by Europeans.

THE EUROPEAN INVADERS

THE FIRST EUROPEAN TO SEE THE MOUTH OF THE AMAZON WAS THE SPANISH EXPLORER AMERIGO VESPUCCI IN 1499. HE DID NOT LAND, BUT IN 1500 A PORTUGUESE SAILOR, PEDRO CABAL, LANDED FURTHER SOUTH AND CLAIMED BRAZIL AS PORTUGUESE TERRITORY.

By 1534 THERE WERE twelve Portuguese settlements along the coast of Brazil, including one at the mouth of the Amazon. The settlers cleared the forest and set up sugar-cane plantations and cattle ranches. They exported wood, sugar and meat to Portugal. The Tupi Indians who lived on the coast were captured and made to work as slaves on the plantations. Those who protested were murdered. Many Tupi were killed by European diseases, such as smallpox and influenza. They had never come into contact with these diseases and had therefore built up no immunity against them. It has been estimated that by 1700, the Indian population of Brazil was only one-third of what it had been 100 years earlier.

▲ *Travelers on the Amazon at the beginning of the nineteenth century. The river journey was hazardous and slow, but it was the only way to reach the interior of the forest. Even today, many villages can be reached only by boat.*

SLAVES FROM AFRICA

The surviving Tupi fled deeper into the forests along the southern tributaries of the Amazon. Once out of reach of the Europeans, they could survive by following their traditional way of life. The supply of Amazonian Indian slaves began to run out. By 1600, slaves were being brought from Africa to work in Brazil. About three million African men, women and children were shipped to Brazil as slaves from 1600 to 1888, the year that slavery was abolished.

Explorers were venturing further into the Amazon forest. The first voyage down the Amazon from Peru to the Brazilian coast took place in 1541 (see pages 16–17). It was followed by exploration in canoes along the tributaries. The Portuguese realized how valuable forest hardwoods such as mahogany, which does not rot, and brazilwood, used to make dye, were. There was a market in Europe for spices from the forest like cloves and cinnamon. Turtles were also valuable. Captured Indians were sent into the forest to kill turtles for the profit of the European settlers.

In the nineteenth century in Europe and North America rubber was found to be a useful raw material for industry. This brought a new wave of exploitation as Amazonian Indians were sent into the forests to "tap" the wild rubber trees. They lived in camps run by the rubber companies and were ill-treated and poorly fed. Thousands of Indians died. But trading in rubber made huge fortunes for the companies who sold it to North America and Europe.

KEY HISTORICAL DATES

1499	First sighting of the Amazon by Europeans
1500	First European landing in Brazil
1541	First European voyage down the Amazon
c.1600	First slaves brought to Brazil from Africa
1822	Brazil became independent from Portugal
1880s	Start of the "rubber boom"
1888	Slavery abolished in Brazil

▶ *This group of Brazilian children illustrates the rich mixture of races among the country's population. Native South Americans, Portuguese settlers and slaves from Africa intermarried. In the twentieth century the mixture has been enriched by over one million Japanese.*

MIXTURE OF PEOPLES

Many Portuguese settlers had children by the Amazonian Indian and African women slaves, and these children grew up to be free citizens. The result is that many Brazilians are mixed race – part European, part Indian and part African. But in the deeper areas of the forest in Brazil there are about 150,000 Amazonian Indians who live much the same kind of lives as their ancestors did before the European invaders came.

TALES OF THE AMAZON

ALTHOUGH BRAZIL WAS PORTUGUESE TERRITORY, IT WAS A SPANISH EXPLORER WHO FIRST TRAVELED DOWN THE AMAZON AND GAVE THE RIVER ITS NAME.

▲ *This model of Francisco de Orellana is in Trujillo in Spain. He died at sea in 1546 while on a voyage of conquest to Amazonia. A town on the Napo river in Ecuador is named after him.*

IN 1540, GONZALO PIZARRO, with Francisco de Orellana as his second-in-command, set out from what is now Ecuador to explore the country to the east of the Andes. After a terrible journey across the mountains, they reached the Napo river, exhausted and short of food. There, the party split up after 20 months. Pizarro decided to turn back with most of the men, but de Orellana decided to carry on with about 100 men. They spent two months building a boat from forest timber. In order to eat they had to kill their horses and they used the horseshoes to make nails.

LEATHER SOUP

In the spring of 1541 they set off. The boat could carry only 50 men, so the fittest had to follow along the river bank. When food ran short, the followers were left behind and were never seen again. The little boat was almost crushed by rapids during a terrifying voyage down the Napo river, but finally de Orellana reached the fast-flowing waters of the Amazon. However his troubles were not over. When the men moored their boat in order to gather food, they were attacked by Amazonian Indians and had to flee. Food ran so short that they had to boil their belts and the soles of their boots with herbs to make a kind of leather soup. At last, in August 1541, they reached the Atlantic Ocean and made their way along the coast to a safe harbor.

De Orellana was rewarded by the King of

WOMEN WARRIORS

It was Francisco de Orellana who gave the Amazon its name. When he returned home he told a story of having been attacked by a tribe of women warriors who reminded him of the Amazon female warriors in the stories of Ancient Greece. So he called the river "the river of the Amazons." But no one else has ever seen the women warriors of the Amazon, and it is likely that what the Spaniard saw was a group of Yagua tribesmen in their native costume, which could have been mistaken for a kind of skirt.

Spain with permission to conquer the land he had discovered, but he died before he could do so. Nearly 100 years later, in 1638, a Portuguese explorer, Pedro Texiera, traveled the Amazon in the opposite direction, from east to west, and claimed it for Portugal.

THE SNAKE CANOE

Most peoples in the world tell stories about how the Earth came to be made and populated. The Tukano Indians, who live in the upper reaches of the Negro river, believe that the Earth was created by the Sun Father, who then sent people to live there. They traveled in a canoe made out of the skin of a giant anaconda, which took them along the rivers and into the forests.

The Tukanos told their story about a creature they knew well. The anaconda, a giant snake that can measure up to 29.5 feet (nine meters) in length, lies almost submerged in the river waiting for its prey. It kills its victims by squeezing them to death, just as the boa constrictor, a member of the same family of snakes, does. The anaconda is not easy to catch and kill, but Amazonian Indians prize it for food and for its tough skin.

▼ *An anaconda at rest. When it is hungry, it will uncoil itself and lie still in the water with only its eyes above the surface. Many stories are told about anacondas attacking fishermen, but it is rare for anacondas to attack humans unless they are being hunted.*

OUT OF THE ANDES

ALTHOUGH, OUTSIDE BRAZIL, THE NAME "AMAZON" IS USED FOR THE WHOLE RIVER, TO BRAZILIANS THE AMAZON IS ONLY THE LOWER 932 MILES (1500 KILOMETERS) BETWEEN THE NEGRO RIVER AND THE SEA.

▶ *This false-color satellite image shows the source of the Apurimac which later becomes the Amazon. It is marked in red above the large white mountains on the left. In 1996 an expedition identified a glacier in this area as the true source of the Amazon.*

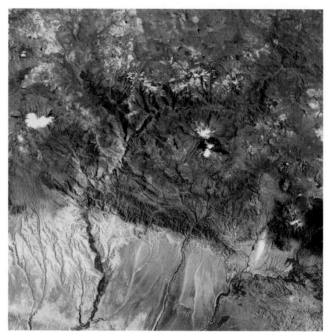

▲ *The Agua Calientes, a mountain stream in Peru whose water flows into the Amazon.*

▶ *In the Apurimac valley in Peru, Quechua Indians make 'chuno', which is dried potato. Here you can see the potatoes drying in the sunlight.*

ABOVE ITS CONFLUENCE, or meeting, with the Negro river, the Amazon has a variety of local names. It starts life as the "Apurimac," whose source is over 16,404 feet (5000 meters) up in the Andes near the town of Cailloma in southern Peru. This is an area of very heavy rainfall – up to 236 inches (6000 millimeters) a year – brought by storms across the Pacific Ocean.

As the Apimurac flows north out of the Andes, it falls over 16,404 feet (5000 meters) in the first 621 miles (1000 kilometers) of its course. It flows down deep canyons, some of

which are over 5905 feet (1800 meters) deep, and crashes over rapids, sweeping boulders and smaller pieces of rock along with it. These rocks gradually erode in the tumbling waters and form part of the sediment that will eventually end up in the Atlantic Ocean.

THE ANNUAL FLOOD

When it reaches the lower slopes of the Andes, the river changes its name and becomes the "Tambo." There are a few settlements here.

The local people graze llamas on the hills for wool and meat and they clear patches of land to grow potatoes, maize and manioc.

The name of the river changes again to the "Ucayali." Here the rainy season lasts from November until June and so there are frequent floods. The rain causes the Ucayali to widen to over three miles (five kilometers).

FARMING BESIDE THE RIVER

The annual flood is vital for the settlements along the river. When it subsides, it leaves behind a layer of mud that improves the land for growing crops. Away from the river, farming is more difficult. Without the new, rich sediment left behind by the floods, the land can be used for only a few years before its plant nutrients are exhausted and a new patch of land has to be cleared.

HEADING EAST

The Ucayali, which so far has flowed north, gradually turns towards the east, heading for the Atlantic – a journey of over 2485 miles (4000 kilometers). At Nauta in Peru, one of the Amazon's major tributaries, the Marañón, joins it from the west. Swollen like the Ucayali with mountain water, the Marañón is a wide river with hundreds of side-streams and islands. About 186 miles (300 kilometers) downstream is the first large settlement on the river, the city of Iquitos.

FRUIT AND VEGETABLES
The main crop grown by Amazonian Indian farmers is manioc, but they also clear small patches of land to grow fruit such as bananas and pineapples, and vegetables like beans, sweet potatoes and peppers. They keep their land fertile with ashes from their cooking fires, and also by breaking up nests of termites. Termites are white ants that live in large colonies in the forest.

ACROSS THE BORDER

AT IQUITOS, THE RIVER
CHANGES ITS LOCAL NAME
AGAIN AND BECOMES THE
AMAZON, BUT ONLY AS FAR
AS THE PERU/BRAZIL
BORDER, WHEN IT BECOMES
THE "SOLIMOES."

▲ *Traditional hollowed-out canoes are the usual form of transport for many Amazonian Indians.*

IQUITOS IS THE HIGHEST POINT on the Amazon that can be reached by ocean-going ships. The first steamship arrived in 1899, in time to open up the river as a route for the rubber trade, which was then at its height. But within 20 years, exports of Amazon rubber were falling because Malaya was producing rubber more cheaply. Iquitos settled down to a quieter life trading with other ports along the river. With the development of oil and mineral exploration in the upper Amazon (see pages 40–41), the port has become busier again, and in the past fifteen years its population has almost doubled to 350,000.

RIVER TRANSPORT

Iquitos is a large city surrounded by untouched rainforest, which is only about 31 miles (50 kilometers) away. There are no road or rail links with the rest of Peru. The only communications are by river or air. River transport is important, not only for trade but also for everyday life. Amazonian Indians use hollowed-out, or "dug-out," canoes to get about. For people without boats of their own there is a variety of ferries, small passenger boats and local boats with palm-roofed awnings to protect passengers and cargoes from the rain and sun.

River traders call regularly at the riverside settlements to collect forest products that they will sell in the town markets. Along the river bank, some Amazonian Indian families live in houseboats and, when the floods come, float with the current to new moorings. Others build timber homes with roofs made out of thatched palm leaves. These houses are built on stilts or wooden platforms to keep them away from the high flood level.

▲ *A fishing village near Iquitos in Peru. The houses are built on rafts and moored so that they will float on the floodwater.*

RIBBON OF WATER

Downstream from Iquitos the Amazon becomes a broad ribbon of water measuring up to six miles (ten kilometers) in width. It can be even wider when it floods. At the height of the rainy season the river can be 121 feet (37 meters) deep. Sometimes the river divides into two streams, flowing past islands that are submerged in the floods.

About 435 miles (700 kilometers) downstream from Iquitos, the Amazon crosses from Peru into Brazil. Three South American countries meet at this point, with their borders running along tributaries of the Amazon. To the north, the Putumayo river separates Peru from Colombia. To the south, the Javari river marks the border between Peru and Brazil. For about 93 miles (150 kilometers), Colombia has its southern border on the north bank of the Amazon before the border veers away northwards in a straight line. For the rest of its journey to the sea, the Amazon is Brazilian.

▶ *A tapper collects latex, which is the milky fluid used to make rubber. A shallow slit is cut in to the bark of the tree to release the latex, which is collected in a cup. The tapper is wearing an oil headlamp so that he can work in the evening when the flow of latex is greatest.*

THE RUBBER BOOM

The Amazon rubber boom lasted from about 1880 to 1915. It brought growth and wealth to the three ports of Iquitos, Manaus near the meeting of the Amazon with the Negro river, and Belém at the Amazon's mouth. By 1912, there were 190,000 Amazonian Indians in the forest tapping wild rubber trees for their latex, or raw rubber. That year, they produced 38,000 tons. But the success of the Amazon rubber trade was short-lived. In the 1880s, seeds from Brazilian rubber trees were taken to Sri Lanka and Malaysia and grown in plantations, where they flourished. By 1915 this plantation rubber was found to be better and cheaper than the wild variety. The great days of the Amazon rubber trade were over, although today there are still 100,000 tappers at work in the forest, gathering rubber for Brazil's own use.

THE BLACK RIVER

ALMOST 3107 MILES (5000 KILOMETERS) FROM ITS SOURCE, THE AMAZON IS JOINED BY ITS MOST IMPORTANT TRIBUTARY, THE NEGRO RIVER. THE NEGRO'S SOURCE IS IN THE HIGHLANDS OF COLOMBIA AND IT FLOWS FOR 1491 MILES (2400 KILOMETERS) BEFORE IT MEETS THE AMAZON IN THE DENSEST PART OF THE RAINFOREST.

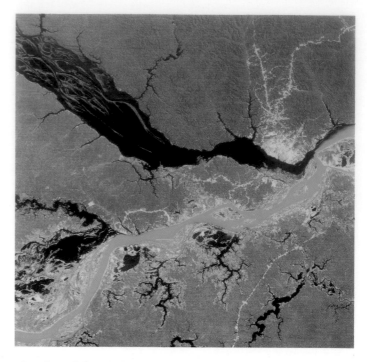

▲ *This false-color satellite image exaggerates the contrast between the color of the Rio Negro, in the top half of the picture, and the Amazon. Manaus is the blue-white area on the north bank of the Negro just before the rivers meet.*

MEASURED BY THE VOLUME of water that pours along it, the Negro is the second largest river in the world, the largest being the Amazon. The Negro carries three times as much water as the Mississippi. The Portuguese named the river the "Rio Negro," or Black River, but its water is brown, the color of strong coffee. The color comes from the rotting fallen leaves of the forest. The Amazon gets its milky coffee color from the sediments that it carries down from the Andes. The source of the Negro is among harder rocks, which do not wear away so easily. Where the Negro and the Amazon meet the two different colors of each river run alongside each other for about 50 miles (80 kilometers) before they merge.

THE FLOOD PLAIN

For the last 497 miles (800 kilometers) before it joins the Amazon, the Negro flows across an almost level plain. Sandbanks and islands form in the dry season, from October to late February. At the height of the floods, in June, the river reaches a width of over 18 miles (30 kilometers).

On the north bank of the Negro, 12 miles (20 kilometers) before it meets the Amazon, is the city of Manaus. It is one of the most isolated large cities in the world. It is unusual to find a city of over one million people surrounded by thick rainforest and 497 miles (800 kilometers) from any other town with a population of more than a few thousand. There is just one road north, and another – that can be used only in the dry season – south. The only other links are by river or air.

◀ *The meeting of dark waters of the Rio Negro, on the right, with the lighter-colored water of the Amazon.*

> ## MANAUS OPERA HOUSE
> The magnificent Opera House was built 100 years ago with stone brought from Europe. Neglected for many years, it has now been restored as a tourist attraction.

FREE TRADE AREA

The rapid growth of Manaus began in 1966 when the government made it a "free trade area." This meant that cargoes landed or loaded there and companies starting businesses did not have to pay taxes. Japanese electronics industries and motorcycle companies moved in. The "free trade" laws meant that the prices of goods assembled locally, such as cameras, watches and radios, were lower than elsewhere in Brazil. So Manaus became a major shopping center despite the distance Brazilians had to travel to get there. For visitors from overseas, travel companies developed "nature tourism" – taking tourists by river or road to the heart of the forest. New hotels were built for the tourists. Then, in 1986, oil and natural gas were discovered 373 miles (600 kilometers) from Manaus near the Urucu river, one of the Amazon's southern tributaries. The oil is pumped for 37 miles (60 kilometers) to the Urucu river, where it is loaded on barges and taken to Manaus to be refined.

◀ *Loading and unloading river ferries on the Rio Negro at Manaus. Despite its development as a modern city, Manaus still depends mainly on the river for communication with the outside world.*

THE LOWER AMAZON

GROWING STEADILY WIDER, THE AMAZON TAKES IN THREE MAJOR TRIBUTARIES FROM THE SOUTH, THE TAPAJÓS, THE XINGU AND THE TOCANTINS, AS IT COMPLETES ITS JOURNEY TO THE ATLANTIC.

THE LOWER AMAZON was the first area of the river to be settled by the Portuguese. In the past 40 years development to the south of the lower Amazon has caused the greatest damage in the whole Amazon basin (see pages 30–31). It began with the building of the Belém to Brasília Highway in 1960, and was followed by the building of the Trans-Amazonian Highway, which crosses the region from João Pessoa and was opened in 1973. These were the first roads to 'open up' the forest, and soon clearance gangs were moving along them to bulldoze the trees.

THE IRON MOUNTAIN

The most destructive single project in the Amazon began by accident. In 1967 an American geologist's helicopter had to make a forced landing on a hillside at Carajás near one of the higher tributaries of the Xingu river. He found that he was standing on an iron mountain. Surveys showed that there were over 18,000 million tons of iron ore in

▲ *Water from the Tocantins river races down a spillway at the Tucurui Dam. The spillway carries away excess floodwater that has built up behind the dam.*

the area – the largest known deposit in the world. There were also valuable deposits of manganese, copper and bauxite – the ore from which aluminium is made.

MASSIVE DEVELOPMENT

This was the starting-point for a huge industrial development. Work began on the Carajás mines in 1982. The Tucurui Dam, the world's fourth largest, was opened in 1984 across the Tocantins river to supply hydro-electricity for the mines.

New homes had to be found for about 20,000 people because their old homes had disappeared beneath the dam's reservoir. A railway was built from Carajás to the Atlantic coast at São Luis, where the building of a new port and the railway terminal led to the relocation of another 20,000 people. All these projects, as well as the demand for land for houses, iron foundries, aluminium smelting plants, roads and power lines, are estimated to have destroyed or damaged the forest over a radius of 186 miles (300 kilometers) from Carajás. In addition, iron is extracted from the ore in furnaces burning charcoal, so there will be a continuing demand for forest wood. People looking for work rushed to Carajás from all over Brazil, and a ring of shanty towns – streets of homes made out of scrap material like plastic sheeting and old iron – sprang up near the site.

The massive development at Carajás was not only Brazil's responsibility. Thirty-three per cent of the costs of the project were met by loans from abroad, including loans from the European Community, Japan and the United Nations' World Bank. Foreign countries, too, were the main customers for metals from Carajás. In return for the European Community loan, EC countries were able to buy Carajás iron ore at very low prices.

▼ *The iron-ore mine at the center of the Carajás Project on the Tocantins river. Brazil is the second largest producer of iron ore in the world, after Australia.*

▲ *The wood-pulp mill that is the centrepiece of the Jari River Project on one of the Amazon's northern tributaries. Set up to exploit the forest to make paper, packaging and building-board, the Project has not made a profit in the twenty years of its life, despite massive investment. The cost of setting up and running the project was far greater than had been planned.*

SYLVESTER MIDDLE SCHOOL LIBRARY

THE MOUTHS OF THE AMAZON

AFTER ITS JOURNEY ACROSS SOUTH AMERICA FROM THE ANDES, THE AMAZON REACHES THE ATLANTIC OCEAN ALONG A NETWORK OF CHANNELS FLOWING THROUGH THE SEDIMENT IT HAS CARRIED DOWNSTREAM OVER MILLIONS OF YEARS.

◄ The Amazon's most easterly tributary, the Tocantins, near Belém. Patches of the rainforest in this area have been cleared, but most of it is still intact.

▼ Marajó Island's forests meet the water. The interior of the island is grazing land.

THOUSANDS OF ISLANDS

THESE CHANNELS are called "the mouths of the Amazon." They cover a distance of 205 miles (330 kilometers). There are thousands of islands between the channels. Each year, when the floodwater arrives, the current eats away at the edges of the islands, carrying the sediment away and depositing it elsewhere. New sandbanks and islands gradually build up, which are constantly changing shape. However, the Amazon does not deposit all its sediment at its mouths. As far as 186 miles (300 kilometers) out in the ocean, the color of the river water can still be seen. It was the sight of the river water that first led the Spanish sailor Amerigo Vespucci to discover the Amazon nearly 500 years ago.

26

◀ *An open-air Sunday market in the center of Belém, which caters mainly to tourists.*

▼ *Belém's fleet of fishing boats works in the creeks and channels of the mouths of the Amazon as well as in the Atlantic.*

Largest river island

The largest of the islands at the mouths of the Amazon is Marajó. It is the world's largest river island. Marajó is almost entirely populated by huge herds of water buffalo grazing on land that has never had forests. Under the Brazilian government's new "Real Plan," introduced in 1995 (see page 42), ranching on Marajó has been singled out as the kind of development that does not involve the destruction of forest and so it will be encouraged in the future.

River defenses

On either side of the mouths of the Amazon are two cities, Macapá to the north and Belém on the south bank of the Tocantins. These were the first cities to be founded on the Amazon. They were built as forts to defend the early Portuguese settlers against attack from the sea at a time when many of the countries of Europe were looking for new lands to conquer.

Macapá is a city of 177,000 people. Belém has a population of 1.25 million, and is the main port at the mouths of the Amazon. It was once the center of the slave trade, and large numbers of people of African descent live in and around the city.

Like Manaus, Macapá and Belém boomed and then slumped with the rise and fall of the Amazon rubber trade, but since the road-building program of the 1960s and 1970s, both cities have prospered again. The Belém-Brasilia Highway (see page 30) links Belém with the capital and the more wealthy southeast of Brazil. The Northern Perimeter Highway (see page 30), which, when completed, will follow Brazil's northern border as far as Peru, begins at Macapá. A large proportion of the machinery and building materials for the Carajás Project passes through Belém, which doubled its population between 1970 and 1980 and had almost doubled it again by 1996.

THE POROROCA

The pororoca is an amazing event that occurs at the northern edge of the mouths of the Amazon every day from January to May when the river is in flood. The meeting of the floodwaters with the ocean produces huge, churning waves that can be up to sixteen feet (five meters) in height, accompanied by a thunder-like roar, which gradually gets louder. Finally, the waves sweep upwards into the river at speeds of up to 15 miles (25 kilometers) per hour.

THE GREAT RAINFOREST

STRETCHING FROM THE ANDES TO THE ATLANTIC, AND
SOUTHWARDS TO THE BRAZILIAN HIGHLANDS, THE AMAZON
TROPICAL RAINFOREST IS THE LARGEST IN THE WORLD. IN FACT,
IT IS LARGER THAN ALL OTHER RAINFORESTS PUT TOGETHER.

◀ This aerial view of the rainforest shows how the emergent trees search for light above the forest canopy. Very little light penetrates through the canopy to the understory and forest floor below.

▼ The taller rainforest trees have "buttressed" trunks, which spread out at the base to support the weight of the tree and to give a large area for the roots. The roots collect nutrients from the soil.

THE AMAZON RAINFOREST is often in the news because large areas in Brazil have been cleared for crops and cattle-ranching. This has been going on since the first Portuguese settlers arrived, but in the past 50 years the pace of clearance has speeded up. Even so, 88 per cent of the rainforest in Brazil – an area the size of France – is still untouched.

THE FOREST CANOPY

Each layer of the rainforest has its own wildlife, and the life of each layer depends on the other layers. The canopy is the "roof" of the rainforest, formed by the tallest trees, for example the jacaranda tree, the brazilwood, the mahogany and the rubber tree. These are often up to 197 feet (60 meters) tall. A few trees grow even taller and rise above the canopy. These are called "emergent trees." The tops of the canopy trees are close together and absorb most of the sunlight. They drop leaves throughout the year and the canopy stays intact through the seasons.

The canopy is home to a huge variety of animal life, including brilliantly-colored butterflies, vampire bats, squirrels, monkeys, and small cats such as ocelots and margays. Birds that live in the canopy include hummingbirds and toucans.

THE UNDERSTORY

Below the canopy is the "understory," where it is dark and moist. If there is a little more light because of a gap in the canopy or along the

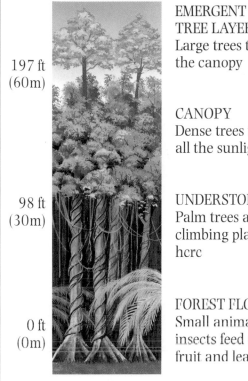

197 ft (60m)	**EMERGENT TREE LAYER** Large trees tower above the canopy
	CANOPY Dense trees take almost all the sunlight
98 ft (30m)	**UNDERSTORY** Palm trees and woody climbing plants grow here
0 ft (0m)	**FOREST FLOOR** Small animals and insects feed on fallen fruit and leaves

THE FOREST FLOOR

Very little light or rainfall ever reaches the floor of the forest. It is inhabited by insects and fungi that feed on dead leaves, and by animals such as armadillos and agoutis. Near clearings and streams, there are grasses and young shrubs. Here deer and tapir come to feed, where they are preyed upon by jaguars.

The tropical rainforest looks so full of plant life that you would expect the soil below to be fertile, but this is not the case. The nutrients in the soil are quickly absorbed by the roots of the rainforest trees, which lie close to the surface of the soil. If the forest is cleared, the soil quickly bakes hard in the hot sun, and even if it is plowed it grows good crops for only a few years.

course of a stream, trees such as palms grow. But the main plants in the understory are small trees that can adapt to the damp, dark conditions. Lianas are climbing-plants that wrap themselves around tree trunks and other plants. Howler monkeys, sloths and jaguars are among the species that live in the understory. Sometimes shrubs grow, making use of any light they can find. If a canopy tree falls, shrubs search for the sunlight and fill the gap left by the tree.

▲ *The toucan is found in the wild nowhere else in the world. Its huge beak, which can be as long as 7 inches (20 centimeters), enables it to eat large fruit.*

◀ *The rainforest atmosphere is so damp that a wide variety of frogs can thrive without living close to rivers or streams. The huge horned frog is found only in the Amazon forest.*

THREATS TO THE FOREST

IN THE PAST 40 YEARS, THE BRAZILIAN GOVERNMENT HAS MADE GREAT EFFORTS TO DEVELOP THE COUNTRY'S VAST NATURAL RESOURCES, INCLUDING THE AMAZON RAINFOREST. SOME OF THESE DEVELOPMENTS HAVE CAUSED WORLDWIDE CONCERN.

TO MAKE MORE USE of the Amazon rainforest, roads were built across it, and businesses were paid to clear large areas of it for growing crops and cattle-ranching. They cleared the forest by burning it, spraying poison from the air, or by huge tractors dragging chains across it. People from Brazil's overcrowded cities were given money to set up small farms. Miners came in to extract the metal ores discovered under the forest and dams were built for large hydro-electric projects along the rivers.

ATTACK ON THE FOREST

This was the biggest-ever attack on the rainforest. A new road was built south from Belém, at the mouth of the Amazon, to the new Brazilian capital, Brasília, across the eastern edge of the forest. This was the Belém-Brasília Highway. Then came the Trans-Amazonian Highway, a 2672-mile (4300-kilometer) long road, built from the Atlantic coast through the heart of the forest to Peru. The Northern Perimeter Highway was another major road, planned to run close to Brazil's northern border and link up with the Trans-Amazonian. It is still only partly built.

Many of these roads are dirt-tracks that have been bulldozed through the forest. In the rainy season, their surfaces are washed away or carried away by landslides. But they are the routes along which thousands of poor Brazilian families have traveled to the forest to find new hope and new lives. Since the plan began, one million people have moved there.

— Trans-Amazonian Highway
— Belém-Brasília Highway
— Northern Perimeter Highway

▲ *A new road cuts its way through the Amazon forest in Brazil. Roads attract landless families from other parts of the country who hope to make a living farming cleared forest land. The poor quality of the land dooms many to failure.*

▶ *Without a covering of trees to protect the earth from torrential rain, the cleared earth of the forest is quickly washed away, leaving the ground unable to support crops.*

THE ATTACK ON THE RAINFOREST

1956: The Brazilian government announces a plan for development of the Amazon forest.

1960: Building of the 1243-mile (2000-kilometer) Belém-Brasília Highway.

1966: The government launches "Operation Amazon" to clear forest for ranching, build dams for hydroelectricity and exploit mineral resources.

1976: Trans-Amazonian Highway completed.

1980: Gold discovered in Amazonia.

1985: First production of iron ore from giant Carajás Project.
Plans for the Northern Perimeter Highway announced.

1995: Brazil's new government announced its "Real Plan" aimed at less damaging development.

1996: Plans dropped for the building of 81 hydroelectric dams in the Amazon basin.

ROADS TO POVERTY

For most, the new roads were roads to poverty. Cleared forest land is too poor to support small-scale family farming. Farmers who could not make a living had to sell their land to ranchers and work for them as laborers. Many had borrowed money to pay for tools and seeds and they were deeply in debt. Violent gangs roamed the forest collecting the money the small farmers owed.

Even for ranching, cleared forest land can be used only for a few years. The soil is not rich enough to replace the grass, and weeds take over instead. Then more land has to be cleared to feed the herds of cattle for a few more years.

PUTTING THINGS RIGHT

The present Brazilian government agrees that mistakes were made in the past. Its policy now is to plan development in the forest more carefully, but there are people who feel that the government could still do more to preserve the rainforest. Some of the damage done in the 1970s and 1980s can never be undone, but with care further destruction can be avoided in the future.

▶ *A farmer struggles to make a living from cleared forest land. It is a desperate fight for survival which many farmers lose.*

THE INDIANS OF THE FOREST

No one knows how many Amazonian Indians live in the forest, because there are areas that have still never been explored by outsiders. Estimates vary between 200,000 and 1,000,000, but most experts think the lower figure is the more accurate one.

There are about 379 different nations, or tribes, of Amazonian Indians in Amazonia. Even this number is uncertain because, from time to time, new groups are found. In 1984, for example, a previously unknown tribe, the Arara, was discovered about 311 miles (500 kilometers) south of the Amazon on the Iriri river.

INDIAN COMMUNITIES

Some Amazonian Indians live in communities alongside people of Portuguese or African descent, working in factories or on farms, or they may join the army. Others live in

▲ *A Yanomami family resting at home during the hottest part of the day. From an early age, Yanomami children are taught the skills that will enable them to survive in the forest.*

reservations – on land that has been set aside for them by the government. About 22,000 Yanomamis, for example, live in an area north of the Negro river, partly in Brazil and partly over the border in Venezuela. Another group, the Tukanos, live higher up on the Negro, near the border with Colombia. The largest tribe in Amazonia, with up to 60,000 people, is the Ashaninka from Peru. Many tribes are very much smaller, and some, like the Arara, consist of just one group or extended family living in one village.

HUNTING AND FARMING

The traditional way of life consists of hunting and fishing for the men, while the women tend the crops and collect medicinal herbs and plants from the forest to sell to river traders. The hunters use bows and arrows, blowpipes or guns. Fishermen trap or net their catch, or release a poison from a vine into the river which paralyzes the fish. Amazonian Indians catch all kinds of game, such as the capybara, which is a large rodent, peccary, a wild pig, and the tapir, a hoofed mammal. They will eat small tree frogs if there is nothing larger about.

MALOCAS

The traditional home of Amazonian Indians is a *maloca*, or longhouse, in which several families live. *Malocas* have mud walls and thatched roofs. Inside, families have their own walled-off sections. They sleep in *hamacas* – an Amazonian Indian invention copied by the rest of the world. This is the origin of the English word "hammock."

UNDER THREAT

All development in the Amazon basin is a threat to the people who live there. They may be forcibly moved off their land, as 351 Parakana Indians were when the Tucurui Dam was built. The environment upon which they depend for survival may be threatened by mining, as is happening to the Yanomami Indians today. Even the mere presence of outsiders, such as settlers or miners, can be a threat to the local people, who quickly fall ill with diseases they have not come into contact with before. Within ten years of the Parakanas

▶ *A Machiguenga Indian village of* malocas *in a clearing in the Peruvian Amazon. This village will house between 20 and 30 families who live in their own sections of the longhouses. All the families come together for the main meal of the day.*

making contact with non-Indians, their numbers had been cut from 1000 to 300 from 1976 to 1986.

Sometimes, the Indians fight back. In 1984, a group of Amazonian Indians on the Xingu river in Brazil kidnapped three government officials and threatened to kill them unless the Indians' land was saved from cattle-ranchers. But with world business anxious to exploit the resources of Amazonia, it looks as if the struggle of the Amazonian peoples to defend their land and way of life will go on.

THE NORTHERN BORDERS

BETWEEN 373 AND 497 MILES (600 AND 800 KILOMETERS) NORTH OF THE AMAZON ARE THE GUIANA HIGHLANDS, WHICH STRADDLE ACROSS BRAZIL'S NORTHEASTERN BORDER AND SUPPLY WATER FOR THE AMAZON'S NORTHERN TRIBUTARIES. THE AREA BETWEEN THE BORDER AND THE AMAZON IS CALLED "CALHA NORTE," THE NORTHERN CHANNEL.

UNTIL 1985, THE CALHA NORTE was a remote region with few roads, cut off from the rest of Brazil by the wide Amazon. Yanomami and Tukano Indians occupied the western half near the Negro river and its tributaries.

THE ARMY'S PROJECT

But in 1985 a plan was put forward to develop the Calha Norte. It came from the army, which was and is still a powerful force in Brazil. One aim was to populate the north as a protection for the border country against invasion from Venezuela or Colombia. Although there have been border disputes with these countries in the past, an invasion of Brazil was in fact unlikely.

The generals planned to set up a chain of military barracks across the Calha Norte,

▼ *These Yanomami Indians have used a black dye made from the juice of the edible genipap fruit to paint their faces. The Yanomomi use this form of face-painting when visiting other Indian communities.*

◀ *The demand in North America and Europe for tropical hardwood from the Amazon was one of the reasons for building roads through the rainforest in the 1960s.*

linked by the Northern Perimeter Highway and a series of airstrips. The cost of these was to be met by selling off the forest for ranching, logging and mining, and by building hydro-electric power stations on some of the rivers.

BUILDING THE HIGHWAY

Work began on the Calha Norte project soon after it was announced. Mining, ranching and timber companies were invited to make offers for the rights to land, and many – including

A PRESENT FROM THE ARMY

Tukano Indians tell the story of an army helicopter that landed in each village in one region and planted concrete markers. This was to show the new borders of the Tukano land, but the soldiers said nothing to the villagers. When the helicopter had gone, most of the villagers pulled up the marker posts and threw them in the river. But one village, in an area without rocks, thought this was a waste and kept their post to use as a washboard!

British and American companies – did so. Work began on completing the Northern Perimeter Highway, although this soon ran into trouble. In the rainy season the new road was repeatedly washed away, and when the land dried out there were landslides and rockfalls. Ten years afterwards, only about one-quarter of the planned route had been built, and most of this had only an earth surface.

The two Amazonian Indian territories of the Yanomami and the Tukano, and the tribal lands of a third nation, the Macuxi, lay right across the route of the road and across some of the land known to be rich in minerals. The army moved the Macuxi on by burning down their homes. One Tukano chief was flown to Brasília and forced to agree to a reduction in the size of the Tukano territory. The Yanomami too lost over half their land, and saw it invaded in 1988 by about 20,000 gold prospectors.

Since the Real Plan was announced, the Calha Norte project and all large-scale development on the Amazon are being reviewed.

TOURISTS ON THE AMAZON

THE BEACHES AND RESORTS OF EASTERN BRAZIL HAVE BEEN POPULAR, ESPECIALLY WITH AMERICAN TOURISTS, FOR MANY YEARS, BUT THE AMAZON IS NOW ATTRACTING TOURISTS.

▲ *Visitors to the rainforest enjoy finding out about the traditional lives of Amazonian Indians, and the national parks run special educational workshops for tourists. Here, a boy has had his face painted and a Yagua Indian in northern Peru is showing him how to load a blowpipe.*

OVER THE YEARS, wildlife television programs and the amount of space given in newspapers and magazines warning about the dangers to the Amazon forest have attracted many visitors to the river.

STAYING IN THE JUNGLE

Tourism provides work, and the Brazilian government is encouraging companies to invest in hotels, transport and other facilities for visitors. International hotel companies have opened hotels in Manaus and Belém, but the biggest growth has been in "environmental lodges." These are usually built deep in the forest and are often reached by river. Visitors to the lodges can study wildlife at close hand. Scientific research stations, too, open their doors to tourists. At one near Iquitos in Peru, visitors can climb up to a "Canopy Walkway," which is a rope bridge erected between the trees 111 feet (34 meters) above the forest floor. Near Manaus, tourists can sleep in a "Tarzan House," which is over 98 feet (30 meters) up in the treetops! Visitors to Marajó Island can stay at one of several buffalo ranches.

Iquitos, Manaus and Belém all have international airports that link in to the world airline network and also connect with other parts of Brazil. Adventurous travelers can also take trips deep into the jungle by small aircraft, where they land on forest airstrips.

RIDING THE RIVER

Most people agree that the most exciting way to visit the Amazon is to travel along the river. Some luxury cruises sail all the way to Iquitos, but they have to stay in mid-channel. Smaller boats can hug the banks more closely and so give passengers a better chance to view the wildlife on the banks of the river. Many boats specially designed for tourists have expert botanists or zoologists on board as guides. Some trips moor for a while so that passengers can go on a jungle trek.

◀ *These Indian boys have captured forest animals to show to tourists. Tourism can sometimes damage the forest environment.*

Of the five Amazonian countries – Ecuador, Peru, Colombia, Venezuela and Brazil – Brazil is the most anxious to attract more tourists from abroad. In the state of Amazonas, which covers the Brazilian Amazon basin west of Manaus, $59 million (£36 million) is to be spent on encouraging "eco-tourism," or nature tourism. The aim in 1996, when there were two million foreign tourists to Brazil, was to double the number within three years.

ECO-TOURISM

Tourism brings work, but it can also damage the environment by the building of hotels and airstrips and by thoughtless exploitation of remote areas and their populations. Eco-tourism is an approach to tourism that welcomes visitors, encouraging them to study and understand the environment and so want to preserve it. Eco-tourism is the fastest-growing sector of the tourist industry in Brazil and Peru.

A CHANGE OF HEART

The Brazilian government's plans for tourism are a sign that attitudes towards the rainforest are changing. The governments of the 1960s and 1970s thought of it merely as land to be used for the greatest profit, whatever damage was done. A thriving tourist trade will help to ensure that enough forest is left for visitors to admire.

▶ *This organized tour along the Tocantins river arranges stops where visitors can study forest plant and animal life at close range.*

THE WILDLIFE OF THE AMAZON

THE AMAZON HAS BEEN DESCRIBED BY A SCIENTIST AS "THE LARGEST COLLECTION OF LIVING PLANT AND ANIMAL SPECIES IN THE WORLD."

ALL THE FACTS ABOUT THE WILDLIFE of the Amazon are amazing. The rainforest is the home of 250 species of mammals, 3000 freshwater fish, 10,000 trees and 70,000 other plant species, 1800 birds, and so many varieties of insects that experts cannot agree on the number. Some say it is 15,000. Others say it is nearer 60 million! New species of wildlife are still being discovered.

FOOD CHAINS

▲ *Macaws roosting and feeding in the forest. Macaws are members of the parrot family. They are caught by South American Indians for food and for their feathers, which are used in headdresses.*

People who look at the teeming life of the rainforest and think about the thousands of species of life in it sometimes find it hard to understand scientists who talk of the rainforest as "fragile." What they mean is that forest life has a very complicated pattern in which species depend on each other for food or shelter. This is called "interdependence."

A food chain is an example of interdependence. In the Amazon forest, the worms, ants and fungi that feed on dead leaves and bark that fall to the forest floor are at the bottom of many food chains. The insects are eaten by the small birds living in the understory. These in turn are caught by some species of monkeys, which live in the forest canopy. Birds of prey, such as the harpy eagle that eats monkeys, live above the canopy in the emergent trees. The chain does not end there. When the eagle dies, it falls to the forest floor and becomes food for insects and fungi. So the food chain becomes a circle.

THE LARGEST ANIMAL

At the top of the food chain is the jaguar, the Amazon forest's largest animal. Although jaguars will climb into the canopy in search of food, they prefer to hunt near streams in the forest for deer, the pig-like peccary and the capybara. If there are enough smaller animals for the jaguar to eat, scientists can be fairly sure that the species further down the food chain are also surviving.

▶ *The jaguar, weighing up to 198 pounds (90 kilograms) and measuring up to 30 inches (75 centimeters) at the shoulder, is the largest member of the cat family outside Asia and Africa. It is the "king" of the rainforest.*

FOOD AND HEALTH FROM THE FOREST

Many foods that we eat or drink came originally from the rainforest. They include bananas, coffee, cocoa, peanuts, cashew nuts, brazil nuts and potatoes. The forest is also the source of many plants that can be used as medicine. Sap from the jaborandi shrub is used to cure some kinds of blindness. Tea made from the leaf of the juca shrub is a cure for stomach pains. The rose periwinkle, which grows only in the Amazonian rainforest, is used in the treatment of leukemia. Amazonian Indians know of hundreds of plants that are used today as the basis of many medicines in the rest of the World.

THE BEE AND THE NUT TREE

Plants and animals depend on each other for more than food. The Amazon rainforest contains a large number of plants called "epiphytes," which live on other plants but do not damage them. One is the orchid plant, which finds a perch, perhaps in the forked branch of a brazilwood tree. The orchid plant is visited by the male orchid bee, which collects pollen on its body that it carries to other orchid plants. The male bee carries a scent that attracts the female bee. She visits the brazilwood flowers and collects pollen in the same way. So the three species depend on each other

◀ *The Amazon is home to the piranha, one of the world's most terrifying fish. Up to 24 inches (60 centimeters) long, piranhas hunt in shoals, or packs, and can kill cattle or humans and strip the flesh from their bones in a few minutes.*

SAVING THE AMAZON

THERE HAS BEEN WORLDWIDE CONCERN FOR OVER 30 YEARS ABOUT BRAZIL'S DEVELOPMENT OF THE AMAZON FOREST FOR CATTLE-RANCHING, CROP-FARMING, MINING AND OIL EXPLORATION.

DEVELOPMENT THREATENED the forest's wildlife. As the bulldozers advanced to clear the trees, species were concentrated into smaller areas. These areas became over-populated and there was greater competition for food. In this struggle, some species were bound to lose, and so did the other species that were dependent on them.

POLLUTED AIR AND WATER

With development came pollution. Vast areas of forest were cleared by burning, which released poisonous carbon dioxide gas into the atmosphere. Scientists warned that this encouraged "global warming," the heating up of the Earth's atmosphere, which was leading to changes in the world's climate.

▲ *An area of the rainforest goes up in smoke. It was this level of destruction that alerted the rest of the world to the danger of global warming.*

▼ *Gold prospectors at work on a tributary of the Amazon. By moving into northern Brazil they have robbed the Yanomami of their land and driven away the fish.*

THE FOREST PEOPLE'S PROTEST

The Amazonian Indians began to fight against development. Some of their leaders visited Europe and the USA to find international help. In 1989, people from about 50 Amazonian Indian groups met at Altamira, on the Brazilian Amazon. They were protesting against a government plan for six huge dams along the Xingu river, which would have flooded thousands of square miles of land occupied by Amazonian Indians. The protest was successful, and the plan was scrapped.

But protest can be dangerous. In the past 20 years, over 50 protesters have been murdered by gangs hired by ranchers. The ranchers wanted to extend their land further and further into the forest. One murdered protester was Chico Mendes, who was killed in 1988 while he was campaigning on behalf of the forest's rubber-tappers. His wife, Izla, carried on the campaign, and later in 1988 the Brazilian government announced the first of a number of areas of forest that were to be protected for rubber-tappers.

▲ *Amazonian Indians traveled to the Earth Summit in Rio de Janeiro in 1992 to protest against the destruction of their homelands.*

Mining for gold, iron ore and other minerals along the Amazon's tributaries did not only destroy the forests. It brought pollution to the rivers, which spread to the Amazon itself. Mineral ores have to be washed before they are refined into metals. Water is taken from the rivers and returned after it has been used. By this time it often contains poisonous chemicals from the refining process. The Jari river, a northern tributary of the Amazon, has been badly polluted by waste from the huge paper-mill complex set up in 1978 and from the china clay mines opened in the area more recently in 1990.

THE EARTH SUMMIT

In 1992 Brazil held the "Earth Summit" in Rio de Janeiro. This was a meeting of nations to discuss problems of the environment that were of concern to them all. It took place in a country that had one of the worst records of environmental damage. The Earth Summit made world leaders think hard about what they could do in their own countries. In particular, it led to a change in the way Brazilians thought about developing the Amazon.

THE FUTURE OF THE AMAZON

IN THE 1990S THERE ARE HOPEFUL SIGNS OF BETTER TIMES AHEAD FOR THE AMAZON FOREST AND ITS PEOPLE.

IN THE PAST, the Brazilian government said that, while it was trying to make the best use of its natural resources, complaints came from countries that had already developed their own resources. So the government was adamant that it would do what it wanted with its own land.

In January 1995, Brazil had a new government with new ideas. These were set out in the *Plano Real* or "Real Plan." The Real Plan promised more care for the environment. One example was the decision to abandon the idea of a series of dams across the Amazon tributaries to provide electricity for Brazil's cities. In the 1980s there were plans for 81 dams to be built by the year 2010, flooding two per cent of the forest and forcing thousands of people to leave their homes. In 1996 the project was scrapped.

RE-PLANTING THE FOREST

As for the forest itself, there are plans to divide it into zones and identify those areas, such as the forest edges, where ranching could be carried on without threatening wildlife. Some areas of forest are to be re-planted, and mining and logging companies will have to plant trees on land that they have cleared. For example, the national oil and gas company Petrobras has set up a seed bank. It will plant 20,000

▲ *A sculpture, the "tree of life," which was exhibited at the Earth Summit in Rio de Janeiro. Made entirely of natural materials, it was a reminder that the Earth's population depends on natural resources.*

trees a year on planned sites in its Urucu river oilfield. The seed bank contains a collection of over 700 species of orchids and other exotic forest plants, which are added when the newly-planted trees begin to grow. As these new forests develop, they will provide habitats for species of animal life that can return to these forests.

Also, on the Jaú river northwest of Manaus, the government has set up the largest rainforest park in the world, which is the size of Israel. To show that it means what it says, the government has closed down some sawmills and other factories using forest products that have not obeyed the new environmental laws.

HELPING HANDS

At the same time, some countries and organizations such as Survival International are giving direct help to the people of the Amazon, often with projects that make life easier for one small community. Aid from Canada, the United States, Germany and Sweden is being spent on projects to help the forest people to sell the goods they produce abroad. In 1996, aid from Great Britain helped Colombia to build a hospital beside the upper reaches of the Rio Negro especially for Amazonian Indian families. There was enough money left over to pay for a boat, which was launched in 1997, to take patients to the hospital by river.

◀ *Herbal medicines gathered in the forest, displayed on a market stall in Belém. Amazonian Indians make medicines from 650 different forest plants.*

▲ *These foresters are going to plant mahogany seedlings in order to restore their numbers in the rainforest. Mahogany is a reddish hardwood that is used for furniture. Millions of trees have been felled and the importance of replanting trees is now recognized.*

GLOSSARY

agouti a small rodent about the size of a rabbit which lives in forests and eats fruit, nuts and leaves

Amazonia the region in South America through which the Amazon river and its tributaries flow

ancestors the earliest generations of a family

awning canvas or plastic sheet to shade people from the sun or rain

botanist a scientist who studies plants

brazilwood a tropical tree with hard red wood used to make furniture; also a source of red dye

capybara the largest rodent, about the size of a pig

cinnamon a tree whose bark is used as a spice in cooking

cloves tropical trees whose buds are dried and used as a spice

confluence the point at which two or more rivers meet

current the flow of water in a channel

descendants people of later generations in the same family

epiphytes plants that grow on other plants but get moisture and food from the air

false-color satellite image a photograph taken from space that uses unnatural colors to highlight certain features

global warming an increase in the temperature on Earth caused by changes in the gases that make up the atmosphere

harpy eagle a very large black and white tropical eagle

howler monkey a large monkey with a loud howling cry

immunity protection from disease which the body builds up naturally by exposure to the disease, or from medicines called vaccines

influenza a feverish disease that can cause serious illness and death if not properly treated

iron ore reddish-coloured rock from which iron is extracted by heating

jaborandi a tropical shrub whose leaves are dried for use as a medicine

jacaranda a tall tropical tree with fern-like leaves and pale purple flowers

latex a milk-coloured fluid produced by the rubber tree

llama hoofed animal of the camel family; it is used as a pack animal to carry people and goods and is also bred for its milk, meat and wool

mahogany a tropical tree with hard reddish-brown wood that is used for furniture

manganese a greyish-white metal extracted from rock and used to make hard steel

margay dark-striped member of the cat family, sometimes called a tree ocelot

meltwater melted ice or snow that flows into streams

nutrients chemicals in the soil that provide food for plants

ocelot large striped and spotted cat with a ringed tail

plantation large area of land where a single crop is grown, such as sugar, cotton or rubber trees

sediment ground-down pieces of rock and other material carried along by a river and later deposited on the river banks and bed

sloth small tailless animal that moves around by clinging upside-down on to the branches of forest trees

smallpox a serious disease that causes fever and spots, which turn to blisters, on the skin

sweet potatoes tropical climbing-plants grown for their yellow fleshy roots, which can be cooked and eaten

tapir hoofed, shy mammal that is about the same size as a donkey; it lives in forests and eats plant shoots and twigs

water buffalo dark gray animal with large horns, kept for meat and as a working farm animal

wilderness area where there is no sign of human interference

zoologist a scientist who studies animals

INDEX